CW00517379

4 ç....

By Judit Brody

An Old Lady Remembers

Lost draft copy of Mary's recollections

In Scotland

Mary Somerville wrapped herself in a plaid rug and pulled a chair up to her desk. She chose her best pen, dipped it in ink and started writing.

This is the story of my life as I remember it. I was born on Boxing Day in 1780. Then she stopped. She thought to herself: 'This is not right, this is not how I remember it. I don't remember being born. Does anybody remember being born or being a baby? I doubt it. But I was told the story so many times that I am beginning to think that I remember it all. How my mother was ill and couldn't nurse me. And how I didn't have to starve because luckily my auntie had a baby at the same time. She had plenty of milk for both of us, so she nursed me and my cousin as well. But I cannot claim to remember this. Better start all over again.'

She crossed out the first two sentences and wrote: This is the story of my life. Well, this is not what she wrote. She actually wrote *Personal recollections* that was published as a book (and she wrote a lot more besides). But let's just keep to her story.

Mary drew the rug tighter around her shoulders. The fire was burning brightly but she was still shivering. Her hands were cold and shaky. She was very old. But she had to keep writing, she wanted all the young girls to know that if they really want to do something, they could do it. She did.

It was not easy for her, but she would have been miserable otherwise.

Her memories crowded her brain.

'We lived in Scotland, not far from Edinburgh. My father was a sailor,

captain of a fifty-gun ship! When he was away at sea nobody kept a close

eye on me. What did I do? I played in the garden, went to the beach all

on my own and watched the birds. I picked shells and ended up with a

nice collection. Then, I had to help around the house, feed the chickens,

shell peas and beans. Mother taught me to read but she did not teach me

to write.

When I was nine years old, one day when father came home from the sea

he made a great fuss. He found out that I could not write. So he packed

me off to boarding school.

I hated school. I cried every day. The food was horrid and we had to clear

our plates.

School Dinners'
finest slop.

Some things havent changed then.

The girls were an unfriendly lot. But the backboard and the stocks were the worst, they made me really miserable. I had a nice straight back so why did they think I needed a board on my back to keep me straight? And the board was not just strapped onto my back, straps were fastened around my shoulders and a plate under my chin to hold my head back. I had to stand in a contraption called the stocks, to have my feet turned out. They wanted to make a lady out of me and ladies were supposed to waddle like ducks. For long hours I had to study standing up in these horrid fetters.

Thank goodness I only had to stay for one year. I learnt to write but never learnt to spell. How ashamed I was when people mocked me for writing "bank knot" instead of "banknote".

To tell you the truth, I still cannot spell, see if you can spot any spelling mistakes in this book (But so far she was only thinking, she did not actually write a book). Anyway, it was lovely to be at home again. Not that I was lazy. I practised the piano every day. But I thumped the keys so hard that some of the strings broke. At the back of beyond, where we lived, there was no one to mend them. I had to mend them myself and I also had to tune my piano. It must have been out of tune much of the time.

In the evenings all the women in the house just sat around, chatting and working on their embroidery. I liked needlework and soon was so good at sewing that I made my own clothes and mended all the sheets and shirts for the whole family.

In the winter we went to Edinburgh and to dancing school. The dancing master called out: "Walk!" He walked alongside us and propped up our chins with his little stick. "Hold your head up high" he said. Sometimes he placed a cushion on the top of our head and we had to walk straight, without letting the cushion fall. He taught us how to curtsey, in case we ever met a member of the royal family.

We had lots of parties. One day I was invited to a tea-party, it was quite boring and I started leafing through some magazines that were on the table. They were women's magazines and they were full of puzzles. Some of the puzzles I didn't understand at all, they had funny lines and there were all these x-s and y-s in the text. I was told it was algebra.

I had an idea. My brother had a tutor, a nice young man, I liked him. Maybe he liked me too. Anyway, I asked him to buy me books from which I could learn about algebra and about geometry. Oh, yes, I forgot to mention, the magazine that I was looking at when I was so bored at the tea-party, had geometrical puzzles too.

Now, why didn't I buy the books myself, you may ask. Because a girl like me couldn't possibly go into a bookshop and buy a book. That was unthinkable. It was so unthinkable that I didn't even think of it.

I got the books.

Now I had a problem: where and when to read them? I didn't want anybody to know what I was doing. I took some candles up to my bedroom and read in bed at night. This was a pretty dangerous thing to do. I could have fallen asleep with the candle burning and it could have set fire to the house! But I never fell asleep because, the books were so interesting. Sometimes I had to put on an extra bed-jacket to stop my arms from becoming blocks of ice.

Then disaster struck! One fine day there were no more candles in the cupboard. Mother got upset: How can that be? We bought enough candles to last for another couple of months.' I kept quiet. A big search started: maybe the candles were put into the wrong cupboard, or maybe somebody had stolen them? But nothing was found until guilty evidence of half-burnt candles came to light in my room and I had to confess.

The upshot was that my candles were taken away and I was forbidden to read. Father was convinced that I would get sick if I studied.

Mary put the pen down. Remembering this incident made her feel sorry for herself. But she was not the kind of person to feel sorry for herself, so she thought it was time to quit writing for the day. She was tired too. And the fire was getting low. Time to have a snack and then to bed.

Mary's secret diary

DEAR DIARY
I HAVE GOT THE SCIENCE BOOKS I WANTED! BUT I DIDN'T KNOW WHERE TO READ THEM. I DIDN'T WANT ANYONE TO KNOW WHAT I WAS DOING. THEN I HAD AN IDEA

I WOULD USE CANDLES AT NIGHT! THE BOOKS WERE SO INTERESTING AND NO ONE SUSPECTED A THING

BUT TODAY MUM SAW THAT ALL THE CANDLES HAD GONE. SHE VOWED TO FIND THEM

Detective Mum on 'The Case of the Missing Candles'

Where are those candles?

BUT UNFORTUNATELY SHE SOLVED THE CASE. UNDER MY BED SHE FOUND.....

HAPPY SHOPPER BURNT-OUT CANDLES

NUTS!

Experiments

The next morning was crisp and clear and cold. Mary settled by the window and on a clean sheet of paper she wrote:

I got married. That was all she wrote and then she just gazed out of the window. 'This was not a very happy time of my life' she thought. Better skip the next few years. 'I had to move to London and I was lonely in that big city. I was shy and never opened my mouth when we were in company. Many times people were talking, saying the stupidest things one could imagine, and I knew that I was in the right and yet dared not say anything. My husband thought that all women were stupid and I was beginning to think so too.

Mary took the pen up again. 'My husband died young and I went back to Scotland. By then I knew that I was not stupid but how could I prove it? I set about studying in earnest. But people started gossiping and soon it seemed that the whole world was laughing at me. "You are wasting your time" was one of the kinder remarks. "She is neglecting her babies, women should look after their babies and not try stuffing their heads with science". I overheard this by chance, but it wasn't chance, I knew that the woman who said this wanted me to hear it.

My babies were fine. We had nursemaids to look after them and I had plenty of time to play with them and to teach them. Gossips could say what they wanted, I couldn't care less. It was my life, not theirs.

And then I married again. I had to move to London. My husband's job paid £300 a year and we were given a house to live in and enough coal and candles to keep the place warm and bright.

But this was different now. My husband, Somerville, he helped me. Oh dear, I am getting forgetful. I should have mentioned earlier that my name was Fairfax. My first husband was called Greig, which means that after I married him I was Mrs Greig, but when I married my second husband then I changed my name to Mrs Somerville.

Anyway, I wasn't a shy young girl any more. I even went to lectures. Going to lectures was all the fashion at that time. At the afternoon tea-parties the talk was always about the experiments we saw. If you didn't go to the lectures you couldn't talk about the experiments and people thought you were dumb.

Then I tried some experimenting myself. We had a lovely sunny garden with a big lawn. I put all sorts of objects on a table in the middle of the lawn. Coloured glass, pearl buttons, salt, pretty much anything I could find in the house, and I watched what happened to them in the sunshine.

Then I set out to show that the rays of the sun have a magnetic effect. I took some sewing needles, I had plenty of those. I needed a prism to separate the violet rays from other rainbow colours in the sunshine. To get a good glass prism was not easy; luckily I could borrow one from a friend. On a fine sunny day I put the shutters on the window, leaving just a chink open. I put my prism there and let the violet rays fall on half the needle. I covered the other half with a sheet of paper. I waited about two hours, I was lucky because there wasn't a cloud in the sky. But I had to be careful because the sun kept moving and I had to keep the violet colour on the needle. All this waiting was pretty boring at first but then it got really exciting. Because at the end of the two hours I tried picking up another needle with the one that had been in the sunshine - and it did pick it up. I proved that sunshine made my needle magnetic!

Well, it was not quite as simple as all that. First of all, I had to make sure before I started the whole experiment that my needle was not magnetic. That is not as easy to do as one would imagine. Then, I had to repeat the experiment many times, hoping to get the same result every time. I also tried using all sorts of other small and thin iron things. My experiment worked every time. So I sat down and wrote about my experiments, sent it to a magazine, and it was published!

This was many years ago. But even now I sometimes wake up in the middle of the night and feel dreadfully embarrassed. It is not something you could see in the dark, but I know that my face is red from shame. Because I was wrong. Now I keep going over it again and again. Where did I make the mistake? Maybe I did not check well enough that the needle was not magnetic when I started the experiment. That is the only mistake I can think of.

I cannot change what happened and it is silly to be embarrassed about it, especially since it happened such a long time ago. I am sure that everyone else has forgotten my shame, except me. It is like having a small dirty spot on your best dress when you go to a party. Nobody notices it but you and it makes you very self-conscious quite unnecessarily.'

Mary felt much better now. Many times in the past she said to herself that it was silly to be so ashamed of a small mistake. Everyone makes mistakes. Now that she has written it down, the horrible feeling seemed to have disappeared. She went for a walk. It was not a long walk; she never went for long walks nowadays, just round the garden. She had a look at the daffodils which were beginning to burst into buds. The snowdrops were nearly over. The fresh air did her good. She was hungry now, it was time for lunch.

Mary had a short nap after lunch and then unexpected visitors turned up. She did her best to be kind and polite to them but she really wished they hadn't come. She wanted to get on with her writing, but the visitors just stayed and stayed and she couldn't find an excuse to get rid of them. And when they finally left, it was too late to start writing again.

She wrote books

The next day Mary got up early and sat down by her desk. She wrote 'How I have changed! It is eight o'clock in the morning, I am already dressed and even had my breakfast. When I was writing my books I stayed in bed until noon, often until one o'clock in the afternoon. I did all my writing in bed. It was warm and cosy there, with plenty of pillows behind my back. But in winter the bedroom was chilly and I had to pile on the woollies. That's how I wrote my book *On the Connexion of the Physical Sciences.* It was a success. Everyone liked it. I gathered together in that book just about everything we then knew about heat, light, electricity, magnetism: all of what we now call science. Of course time has moved on and by now this book is a little old-fashioned but when it was published it was still brand new knowledge. And everyone knew that a woman wrote it because I was not afraid to sign my name. Many women wrote books, good ones, and did not publish them under their own names. Some even pretended that the books were written by their husbands because it was not seemly for a woman to write a book. Like that tedious girl Ada, she just put her initials: A. A. L. at the bottom of her article'

Mary stopped for a second. "I am not well organized" she thought. "I am jumping ahead of myself, writing about things that happened later, before all the things that happened earlier. For example, I wrote the Connexion book after I translated the *Mechanism of the Heavens* and I have not mentioned that one. Who cares, I will write as it comes to my mind. The heavens book I translated from the French. It was written by a famous astronomer called Laplace. I put some additions to it and it was used at Cambridge University as a textbook for students!"

'We went to lots of parties and met lots of interesting people. Mr Babbage gave the best parties. He was funny, but he also grumbled a lot. He always grumbled about the government not giving him enough money to finish his calculating machine. I met Lady Byron and her daughter Ada, at one of Babbage's parties. Lady Byron was the famous poet's wife but they were separated years before and Lord Byron, Ada's father was dead by then.

Ada was just a young girl and she wanted to learn maths and wanted to understand the calculating machine. She kept pestering me with her questions and her letters. But I didn't mind. In my studying days I needed help too and used to pester people with my questions. I decided to be patient with Ada and help her. And she did me proud. She translated an article on Mr Babbage's calculating machine and added her own explanations to it. I read what she wrote and it made me understand Babbage's ideas.

Ada married a good friend of my son. But then she started betting on horses. She may have thought that she had a foolproof system of winning, but all she had was a foolproof system of losing. And then she died so young. But I am sure that if anyone ever makes a calculating machine that works properly, Ada will be remembered.'

Mary stopped writing. Thinking about Ada made her sad. So pretty and so full of life. And clever too. But women always had to fight against the odds.

"We are not even allowed to vote" thought Mary. "Some women got up a petition which I signed too. We were asking the government to give women the vote. And did they? NO. It's not fair.

And why cannot women get university degrees? If they can pass the exams that means that they are as good as the boys and should be given degrees just like the boys. I signed the petition for women to be allowed to get degrees at London University.

What else could I do to help other women? There is this saying that knowledge is power. Maybe if women have knowledge, they will also have power. I could not give women power, but I could give them knowledge. I could tell them about the wonderful new inventions and discoveries.

After all, the world has changed a great deal in my lifetime. For instance, when I was a young girl there were many places on the Earth that we hardly knew about. Now, wonder of wonders, anybody can send a telegram from London and it will get to any of the large Australian towns in a few hours. So I set about explaining all we know about the Earth in my book on geography.

And another thing. Microscopes are so much better now than they used to be. Which means that we know a great deal about tiny, tiny things. There

is a whole world that we cannot see with the naked eye. I explained all we know about the world of small things in my book on molecular and microscopic science. I did my best to give women knowledge. Maybe one day they are going to have power as well.

Author and illustrator with Mary Somerville's bust in Somerville College Oxford

In many parts of the world girls can now study whatever they wish and receive degrees just like the boys.

Somerville College in Oxford was named after Mary Somerville.

An Ambitious Girl

Bumps?

'Mother, please, let me get up!' little Ada was pleading. But nobody heard her because she was all on her own in the room. She kept kicking the cushions at the end of the couch really hard. Lying on a board for an hour seemed like eternity. It was so uncomfortable. Her mother said that it would keep her back straight. But there was nothing wrong with her back. Having to lie on the board was just one of those things some girls had to put up with in those days, some 150 years ago. On top of that, Ada had to study while she was lying there. Well, at least it took her mind off the board.

Ada always did as she was told because she wanted to please the grown-ups. It would have been quite possible to get off the couch without anyone noticing. But this did not enter her head. It would have been too scary to risk detection. And disapproval. So she waited while another million years passed. (Later on you will see that when Ada grew up she changed and became quite headstrong.)

Ada was so board!
(sorry for the rubbish joke).

At last Ada's mother came in. She was not alone. A well-dressed young gentleman followed her. 'How is my little darling?' asked Ada's mother, Lady Byron. Then she saw the cushions all higgledy-piggledy. 'What happened here? Ada, really, you must be more careful next time'. She settled herself in an armchair. 'Come over here, the doctor is going to feel the bumps on your head'.

Ada was glad to be on her feet again, but she was suspicious about those bumps. Did she really have bumps on her head? She rubbed her head with both her hands. She couldn't feel anything.

'Don't mess up your hair'. Lady Byron was beginning to get cross. 'I told you to come over here.' The young man carefully ran his fingers around Ada's skull.

'Her bump of self-confidence is small, we should set about enlarging it' He turned to Ada's mother: 'How is her health?' he asked. 'She is often ill' was the answer.

The young man carried on with his investigation.

'The bump for numbers is strong.' Ada thought that her mother may have told the young man that she loved numbers. Then again, maybe she did have bumps on her head. It made no difference, when they finished with her head she still had to go back onto her board for another hour.

The measles

Sometime after the young doctor's visit Ada woke up in the morning with a splitting headache. Her eyes were red, she was shivering and had a rotten cold. Then her temperature shot up. For days and days she would not get any better. Everyone was awfully worried about her. Then itchy spots appeared all over her body. She had the measles.

Nowadays babies get shots (vaccination) against measles but when Ada was a little girl there was nothing one could do against it, just wait for it to go away. Most children caught measles. Poor Ada was very ill for a long time. And when she finally got better, she had lost the strength in her legs. She simply could not walk.

Lady Byron thought that Ada would get better if she was magnetized. She took her to a magnetic doctor. No, the doctor was not magnetic, but he had a large magnet and he stroked Ada's chest and her back with the magnet. Luckily she was not dressed in a suit made of iron, like armour. In time Ada recovered. Her mother always believed that it was magnetism that cured her. But this is not very likely.

Numbers, numbers, numbers

The clerks, who were called computers, were sitting in a long row, hunched forward. They never tried to lean back because they would have fallen flat on their backs. They were sitting on stools. But actually they were lucky to be sitting. Some others had to stand at their desks all day long. That is why the computers, who were not machines but living human beings, did not complain.

They all had paper, blotting paper, pens and an inkstand. And rows upon rows of numbers. It was only three o'clock but it was already getting dark. Oil lamps and gas-lamps were lit, but even so the room was still dim. The little elderly man sitting somewhere in the middle rubbed his tired eyes. 'Numbers, numbers, numbers, all day and every day. I even dream with numbers' he said. 'I wish someone would invent a machine that could add and multiply. Then we could all go home and sit in the garden.'

'Are you crazy?' another was quick to reply. 'First of all, who wants to sit in the garden in the middle of winter? Then, if a machine does the work, we shall not be needed and we shall get the sack and won't have any money and no garden to sit in. But your machine is only a fairy story anyway. No machine can be made to work out all these numbers.'

'I am not crazy. Mr. Babbage said that he is going to build a steam driven calculating machine. Look at these wonderful steam engines; who would have thought a hundred years ago that locomotives would be built to pull carriages, and that we would be sitting comfortably in the carriages and being pulled along at speeds even as fast as twenty miles per hour? '

'We will not be around in a hundred years' time, if it will take that long to invent a calculating machine. And look out, the supervisor has his eyes on us, we had better get on with our calculations. As the supervisor approached all bent down to their work. They had to work fast and never make a mistake. A mistake could mean a ship running aground, or men drowning; anything could happen. Of course, mistakes were always made: one cannot make hundreds of calculations and never make a mistake. Luckily most mistakes did not cause major catastrophes.

A computer getting home from work.

Mr. Babbage and his parties

Mr. Babbage did not invite the calculating clerks to his parties. They were

grand occasions, with fancy little iced cakes and all kinds of savoury titbits. But the best thing about them was that he always had a surprise in store. Usually some kind of a toy. The very best was a little automatic ballerina made of metal. When it was set in motion, a small bird perching on her hand flapped its wings ready to fly off. But it never flew off. Then the ballerina turned round and round and lifted her leg so that you could see her lacy knickers.

Today's party was special. Ada and her mother were invited. All the other guests were eager to meet them - Lady Byron, wife of the famous poet and her daughter, Ada. Does she look like Lord Byron? Does she limp as he used to? No, she does not. She is very young and pretty.

Ada wanted to meet Mrs. Somerville. Sure, she had to be polite and smile at all the other guests. But when she saw Mr. Babbage she suddenly forgot her smiles and her manners. She was not shy, but went up to him and said: 'Will you please introduce me to Mrs. Somerville? I so want to meet her. You know, she wrote that marvellous book on the heavens. I haven't read it; I don't think I would understand it, but I do want to read it one day. As soon as I have learnt enough mathematics. Maybe she would teach me. Would you teach me?' And she looked up at Babbage with her huge eyes, imploring him to say "Yes".

Babbage smiled. 'All right, all right, I will take you to Mrs. Somerville. But you know, she did not actually write that book, she translated it from the French and only added her own remarks'.

'That's what I mean. She understood enough to be able to translate it. If she could only find the time to teach me!' cried Ada, dancing from one leg to the other in her excitement. She was very nearly jumping up and down. Babbage left the young girl in the company of the older woman and went to his study to get ready the surprise he had prepared for the party. A few minutes later he appeared in the doorway. 'The assembled company is invited to join me and marvel at the calculating machine I made' he announced. They all trooped in and there was no end of AAAH-s and OOOH-s, there may have been a few WOW-s too. There stood the machine, rods and handles, wheels upon wheels, all shiny brass with numbers on them.

They all knew that Babbage had been working on a machine. The government paid him to make a calculating machine. Such a machine was badly needed because although the clerks worked very hard, they always made mistakes. A machine would not make mistakes. One part of the machine was now ready and the party guests were the first ones to see it and to see how it worked.

'Quiet please' ordered Babbage and started turning the handle. 'What should we calculate?'

'Make it simple'- shouted somebody- 'Just add two and two together. Is your machine clever enough to do that?'

The handle turned and the numbers came up: 2 and then 4. Then Babbage said: 'Let's carry on going up in twos. He turned the handle and the numbers appeared in order: 6 , 8, 10, 12... The room was really quiet now. When the numbers reached 48, 50, Babbage said: 'This is getting boring. Why don't we add one hundred and ten to it' and by the next turn of the handle up came 50+110, that is, hundred and sixty.

After the hushed silence there was sudden murmur. 'A miracle' -said Lady Byron- 'A machine that thinks.'

'No, madam' -replied Babbage- 'This went exactly according to my instructions. The machine cannot think. I am the one who can think!'

Correspondence course

'Dear Mrs. Somerville, it was so good of you to help me the other day with my mathematical problems. Could you please help me again? I'm afraid that I am stuck.' Ada was writing yet another letter to Mary Somerville who patiently answered all her queries.

'Dear Mr. Babbage, thank you for your last letter, it was ever so helpful. But today I have another question....'

'Dear Mr. De Morgan, I would like to know the following...'

Ada never tired of writing her letters and asking for help with her studies. She was married now. Her husband was William, the 8th Baron King who became later the Earl of Lovelace, so Ada became Lady Lovelace. Then

Ada had babies and although she had help around the house she was very busy and it was difficult to find time for her studies.

There were some scientists who thought that women have weak bodies and any kind of studying would hurt them. But Babbage was not one of them. He encouraged Ada in her studies and even told her all about his machines. In the end she knew enough to be able to translate an Italian scientist's essay on the calculating machine. She even added her own explanation to it. And she explained what the difference between a calculator and a computer is. (Do you know what it is?)

The trouble was that the famous machines were not ready. They were mostly in Babbage's mind only. People still argue about why exactly Babbage could not finish his machines. He himself was convinced that the government did not give him enough money to finish making them. But the government said that they had already given him more than enough money and were not willing to give him any more.

An argument

One evening Ada was sitting in her spacious living-room, sewing a bonnet. She wanted to give it to her friend Mary Somerville as a present. Mary was an old-fashioned woman, who liked wearing something on her head even indoors. Maybe because when she was young she lived in an old and cold house in Scotland she had got used to having to wrap up even inside the house.

'Listen, William' Ada said to her husband who was quietly reading his book. 'I am furious. Babbage asked me not to publish my paper because he wants to write some sort of a separate introduction to it. He wants to tell the whole world why he has not finished the calculating machine.'

William looked up from the page he was reading and asked Ada 'What are you going to do about it?'

'I have already done something about it' said Ada. 'I wrote him a long letter. Do you know how many pages long?'

'You tell me' replied William. He looked at Ada, then chanced a guess 'Five pages?'

'Come on, you cannot say much in five pages' said Ada, 'My letter is sixteen pages long and I have already sent it this afternoon. I told Babbage that he cannot make me give up now. I worked pretty hard on that essay. I told him that I will help him if he promises not to meddle into my affairs. I might even give him some money to finish his project.'

William thought that she sounded rather bossy. He wanted to change the subject. 'What are you working on?' he asked.

'A bonnet for Mrs. Somerville' answered Ada. 'Look it's nearly ready. Isn't it pretty?? I hope Mary will like it.'

William was happy to approve of the bonnet. He was happy that there was no more talk about giving money to Babbage.

But Babbage was not happy when he received Ada's letter. 'What does she think, giving me orders' he grumbled. 'She used to be so timid, she would hardly open her mouth. And who taught her everything she knows about calculating machines? I did. And anyway, who invented the machine? I did. What did she do? She just wrote about it.'

In the end it was Ada who had her way and published the article. Even so, she was not courageous enough to sign her name. She just put her initials A. A. L. underneath.

What else to do?

For a long time Ada worked very hard on her studies. She worked also on her translations and writing about her own ideas of how to make a calculating machine work. Now she wanted to have some fun. The trouble was (and it is a sad thing, but has to be told) that she started betting on horses. She had always liked horses. She liked riding and going to horse races. But some new friends encouraged her to bet on them. And she did not win. As a matter of fact, she lost. Then she wanted to bet more, hoping to win this time to make up for the earlier losses. She lost again. She did not have any money left and had to sell some of her jewellery. She even had to borrow money to make ends meet.

People say that Ada Lovelace was the very first computer programmer.

A computer language is named after her.

What Is Mathematics?

Childhood in Russia 150 years ago

The blackberries that they picked were delicious! But the two girls, Anya and Sophia, had gone to the woods on their own and without permission. They also ate other kinds of berries that made them sick. When they got home Nanny was angry. She said in a harsh voice: 'Go to your rooms! And stay there!'. Anya hated being imprisoned in her bedroom. Sophia did not mind at all because she loved studying her wallpaper. Studying the wallpaper? Well, the wallpaper in Sophia's room was something special. When the house - really a small palace in the beautiful Russian countryside- was redecorated, the flowery paper ran out before her room was done. So the decorators papered Sophia's room with the pages of a book. The walls were covered with letters and numbers and strange signs. Sophia knew her letters and her numbers, but what were those strange squiggles? They were ever so interesting. She resolved to find out what they all meant. Uncle Peter said it was higher mathematics. But what was higher mathematics?

One beautiful summer day Nanny told Sophia to go out into the garden. Sophia started bouncing her ball, but there were no other children around and soon she got bored. So she crept secretly into her father's library. Maybe she could find out about mathematics. She had no luck, none of the heavy volumes that she carefully took off the shelf had any higher or even lower mathematics in them.

Next time when Uncle Peter and Uncle Fedor came visiting she would ask them. Uncle Peter sat Sophia on his lap and explained about all sorts of different numbers. Odd numbers and even numbers. Square numbers like four and nine and sixteen, the kind that you get when you multiply a number by itself. Uncle Peter told Sophia about prime numbers too, like seven, eleven and thirteen. He said 'Try to divide these by any other number' But try as she might, she could not do it. Uncle Peter laughed 'Prime numbers always leave a remainder, and do you know: there are infinitely many of them'. Then he told her stories about negative numbers which were less than nothing. And imaginary numbers. He talked about different shapes too, and about infinity. Sophia wondered a great deal about infinity as she could not really imagine it.

Uncle Fedor's stories were different. They were about mountains and oceans and the tiny creatures too small for the eye to see, that lived there. Sophia enjoyed Uncle Fedor's stories, but she much preferred the stories about numbers.

Many years later – an idea

'No, no, no' said the General who was the girls' father. 'Girls must not travel on their own. It is unheard of!' His face was quite red. 'But I want to study' wailed Sophia 'and here in Russia the universities will not teach girls'. Anya had another idea. She told Sophia in secret: 'One of us should get married. A married woman can travel with her husband and her sister can go with them, and I know just the right young man, his name is Vladimir Kovalevskii. He wants to go abroad and study fossils.'

Sophia was pretty but she was not sure of herself and did not consider herself to be pretty. She was quite shy. She thought Anya would marry Vladimir, after all she was the older sister. But Vladimir insisted on marrying Sophia.

'What is the world coming to?' muttered the General under his moustache while he was waving good-bye to his daughters and his brand new son-in–law. But in secret he was rather proud of Anya and Sophia. They were serious young women. True, they liked pretty clothes but they had other interests as well. The famous writer Dostoyevsky had already published one of Anya' short stories in a magazine, in fact he had even proposed to her. As for Sophia... who could tell what such a clever girl might do?

When Sophia arrived in Heidelberg she asked to be accepted as a student. In those days very few universities allowed girls in the lecture room, so the professors held a special meeting to discuss whether to let Sophia attend their lectures. At hearing their verdict Sophia ran home to Vladimir and Anya 'They let me in! I am accepted! I am allowed to study!' She was happier than she had ever been in her life.

But Anya had other plans. 'I am not staying in this boring little town. I am going to Paris' she said. 'Life is more exciting there. I want to become a famous writer and a revolutionary'. And she left.

Studying, studying

'Thank you Professor Bunsen' Sophia mustered her sweetest smile. 'So as you will let my friend work in your laboratory, can she be here first thing on Monday morning?'. 'All right, all right, she can start on Monday' said the professor. As Sophia left, the grumpy old man buried his head in his hands and sighed. Everyone in Heidelberg knew that Professor Bunsen had sworn never to let women into his laboratory and this Russian girl had charmed him into eating his words -so to speak. What would his students think now? Many of them were just as prejudiced against women as he was.

Sophia studied maths, physics, chemistry and medicine. The work was hard but she loved every minute of it.

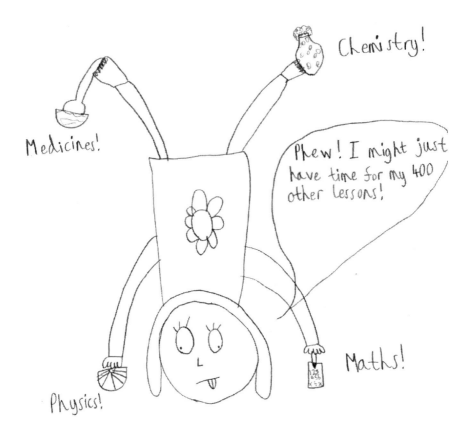

She explained to Vladimir: 'All girls should have the opportunity to study at a university if they want to. But men believe that women are stupid and not good at studying. I want to show that women can be as good at science as men.'

One day she got her chance. The professor of mathematics made a mistake. He looked at his notes, he looked at the blackboard. He scratched his head. There was a long silence. Then the students started giggling. Sophia put up her hand 'Sir, I think I know what the trouble is'.

'Do you now?' the professor sounded doubtful. 'Come on out and show us'. All the other students turned their heads to look at Sophia. But she marched right out to the blackboard, took a piece of chalk and explained where the mistake was. When she finished they all clapped, even the professor. Nobody dared make fun of her after that.

It was not an easy life for the two students Sophia and Vladimir. They had to speak German all day long. How glad they were in the evenings when they could relax and talk to each other in Russian which was their mother tongue. Sophia also had to learn how to do housework. 'I wish I had servants to do the chores, just like at home' she sighed. She was frightfully untidy, could not cook and neglected her clothes. Vladimir was no better. They had plenty to learn.

But they had holidays and travelled around. They came to England and visited the famous writer George Eliot. (You probably know that George was not a man but a woman, whose real name was Marian or Mary Ann Evans.) Sophia had read and liked Eliot's novels and admired her for her courage to live life as she wished. When they met, Sophia found her old and ugly, but her voice was sweet and she was quite charming. In the end Sophia admitted that Eliot was at least ten times as nice as she had imagined.

When Sophia finished her undergraduate studies the professors advised her to study for a doctorate. But where? There were no universities that would accept a woman as a doctoral student. Sophia screwed up her courage and went to Berlin to ask a famous professor to give her private lessons. She put on her best dress and a huge hat. The hat covered her face so that the professor should not see how young she was. 'I do not teach women' grumbled the old bachelor. 'But here are some problems. If you can solve them then I promise I'll take you on'. He thought that a woman would surely not be able to pass his test. Sophia had no difficulty solving the problems and Professor Weierstrass kept his word and agreed to teach her.

Soon Professor Weierstrass realized how talented Sophia was and the two became good friends. They worked together on various problems in mathematical analysis. In one of her studies Sophia made some calculations about the rings of the planet Saturn. Now we think that the rings are made from small pieces of ice and rock. Sophia followed a famous French astronomer who believed that they are liquid and she figured that the cross-section of the rings had to be egg shaped.

After much work Sophia was one of the first women in the world to become Doctor of Mathematics. And with distinction too!

A trip to Paris

While Sophia was still in Berlin a war broke out between France and Prussia in 1870. The German army marched towards Paris and surrounded the city. At the same time a revolution started in Paris. The Paris

Commune. Anya, who was married to a Frenchman, was in the midst of it.

Sophia and Vladimir were terribly worried and decided to visit her. But the

German troops and the soldiers would not let them pass. Should they turn

back and return to Berlin? They looked at each other and said 'We shall

find a way to get to Paris and to Anya'.

They waited until dark and crept through the German lines. Then they

walked along a river bank for a while and found an abandoned boat. As

they started to row, the Germans started firing at them. Luckily the bullets

missed and the fugitives landed safely. When they got to Paris they found

that people there were starving. There was so little food that the Parisians

ate their cats, their dogs, and even rats and mice, if they could catch

them. During the siege of Paris Sophia helped by nursing the wounded.

Back to Russia

When Sophia finished her studies in Berlin, she returned to Russia. But she

was very disappointed when she found out that her doctorate counted for

nothing there. She was not allowed to teach mathematics, not at the

university and not even in a secondary school. 'I am not very good at my

tables' she thought. 'I don't want to teach in an elementary school, the

children would laugh at me if I could not figure out how much eight time

seven make. What can I do now?'

Vladimir told her 'We have studied enough, let's enjoy ourselves'. And they did. They started to give parties and went dancing a lot. They spent money on fashionable clothes. Then Sophia had a baby girl. She named her Sophia, but everyone called her by her nickname Foufa.

'A letter from Germany' announced the postman one day. It was from Sophia's old professor in Berlin. 'Are you working on mathematical problems?' he asked. 'Come back, I shall help you find a job.' Suddenly Sophia realized how much she missed her work. She needed money too. They had spent so much on their jolly life with Vladimir, and also on some bad business deals, that she had to sell her jewelry, even her engagement ring. It was time to get back to work.

Sophia found her old notebooks at the bottom of a big trunk and slowly started to revise everything. She went to lectures and wrote letters full of mathematical problems to her old friends. Then she tried to figure out how light travels in crystals. Unfortunately she made a mistake in her calculations. (This happens more often that you would think in the work of a mathematician.)

Sophia thought 'So many people know so little about the exciting new discoveries and new inventions. They have never heard of the telephone, the typewriter or the flying machines. I shall write about them in the newspapers and I shall explain them so that everyone will be able to understand and marvel at them'. Her articles were well written and the newspapers were happy to publish them.

Soon another letter arrived. 'The new university in Stockholm in Sweden would be honoured if Madame Kovalevskaia accepted a position there.' Vladimir said 'Go, Sophia! You can take Foufa with you. I shall stay in Russia and try to sort things out'. But poor Vladimir could not sort things out. Soon he became very ill and died. Sophia and Foufa were alone in Stockholm. Luckily Foufa had a nanny to look after her so that Sophia could go out and teach at the university.

The professor

Once again, Sophia worked very hard and again she wanted to show that a woman can be as good a mathematician as a man. Her students liked her very much because she was a good teacher. They understood all the difficult theorems because she explained everything so very clearly.

'Foufa, time to go to bed!'

'Just a few more minutes, mother.' The daily argument between Sophia and Foufa sounded louder and louder. 'You know that I have to work and I can only work when you are in bed' pleaded Sophia. She prepared her lectures and did her mathematical calculations when Foufa was fast asleep.

'The French Academy of Sciences is advertising a competition for an essay. The prize money is 3,000 francs' a friend told Sophia. 'I could do with the money' Sophia sighed 'but I haven't got anything ready. My essay is only half finished. I have not time for anything.'

'You had better find the time and get cracking' was the answer.

Sophia finished her essay just in time to meet the deadline. She gave it the title *On the Rotation of a Solid Body about a fixed Point* and sent it off to Paris. It was about a special spinning top and how it moves around. Her calculations can be used for describing the movements of the gyroscope.

The competition was anonymous so Sophia did not have to put her name on the paper. When the judges awarded her paper the first prize, they did not know that it went to a woman. The paper was so good that the judges increased the prize money to 5,000 francs.

Sophia was happy, but very, very tired. Looking after Foufa, teaching at the university and writing scientific papers would be quite enough work for anybody. But Sophia also wrote novels and plays and she always campaigned for women's rights.

She was also homesick for Russia. About her holiday trips home she said to her friend: 'The journey from Sweden to Russia is the most beautiful in the world. When I am on the boat I look at the sea and the clouds, on the train ride I see lakes and mountains and lovely birch woods and waterfalls.

It goes by in a flash. The same journey going the other way, from Russia to Sweden, is slow and boring and it lasts forever.'

One day, just after she returned from holiday, she was invited to a dinner party. But she had a bad cold. 'It is only a chill' she thought. 'I have been looking forward to this party, I don't want to miss it. I just hope that no one will catch my cold'.

But she didn't really enjoy the party. She should have stayed at home and in bed. She became terribly ill. In those days there was no penicillin and there were no other antibiotics to help you fight an infection. Sophia's frail body could not cope without such help and she died of pneumonia.

Sophia Kovalevskaia had a talent for mathematics. She also had a very strong will.

The mathematical methods that she worked out are still useful.

The Experimenter

Hertha (who had recently changed her name from Phoebe Sara) was embroidering a tablecloth for Barbara. Her hands were busy but her brain was even busier. She was thinking about her recent interview. 'I shall be one of the first girls to study at Cambridge. They are building a new college for us. And not only did Barbara Bodichon promise to give me more needlework for which she is going to pay me, but she is going to introduce me to the famous writer George Eliot'. This was about 150 years ago.

So it happened that Hertha Marks, a Jewish girl without a penny to her name, was able to go to Cambridge University. She studied mathematics. She had to work hard not only at her studies but also to earn a living. Some of the money that she made by doing needlework and giving private tuition she sent to her widowed mother and sickly sister. But Barbara was as good as her word and helped her. So did George Eliot (who was really a woman - and you can read a little more about her in the chapter on Sophia) one of whose many novels features a young girl very much like Hertha. People think that George Eliot may have based this character on Hertha.

Fire! There were no smoke detectors in those times and when a haystack caught fire the smoke was thick enough to scare the girls in the college. Hertha decided that they should have their own fire brigade. The firemen laughed: 'What do girls know about extinguishing fires? They can't even scale a ladder.' Can they not? Hertha had always been a tomboy (to her mother's grief). Now was the time to show them what a girl can do. She easily climbed the longest ladder. From then on the Fire Brigade supported the girls' own fire brigade.

After her final exams (women were allowed to take exams but were still not allowed to get a degree) Hertha earned her living by teaching and sewing but her busy mind did not rest. She invented a 'line divider' and patented it (hoping to make a lot of money). This instrument could divide a straight line into any number of equal parts. Hertha did not have enough money to pay for a patent so Barbara Bodichon helped her with that too. Then she decided to study more and enrolled at a technical college. This changed her life because soon she met and married one of the professors who was a widower.

Uses of electricity were just being developed and it was an exciting subject. Come to think of it, it still is exciting. Her husband, Professor Ayrton, experimented with electricity and at first Hertha was happy to help him. One day the professor travelled to a conference in America, while Hertha stayed at home. She carried on experimenting and sent him the results.

During the conference it happened that the professor could not find his notes. 'Where is my paper?' he wondered, 'I left it on this table and it is not here' 'Sir, we thought it was scrap paper and needed it to light the fire' said a servant. Professor Ayrton sighed: 'It was my only copy! What am I to do?' (In those days there were no computers or copying machines). When he returned to England Hertha told him: 'leave it to me, I shall carry on this work in my own name'. The professor agreed because he knew that she was just as capable as he was.

Arc lights

Do not try this at home!

Many people still believed that women were no good at science and that Hertha was only helping her husband. This was not so, it was Hertha who did the work: trying to improve electric arc-lights while her husband was busy doing other experiments. Why was she bothered about them? Because in those days, before electric light bulbs came into use, arc-lights were everywhere.

Arc-lights were the brightest man made lights on earth. They were so bright that they would have harmed your eyes if you looked directly at them. Arc-lamps were used generally for lighting outdoors but also for special purposes such as in cinemas for projecting the pictures. Also, they were very important for the Navy that used them as searchlights.

How did arc-lights work? Two carbon rods just touching (not to be confused with the 'carbon' in the atmosphere which is really carbon dioxide, these rods were like small pieces of pure coal) were connected to electricity, then separated, leaving a little gap between them. To complete the circuit, the arc, like a tiny bolt of lightning, leapt from one rod to the other.

The trouble was that they gave out funny noises and spluttered and often had to be adjusted when parts of the carbon rods burned away. Hertha worked out how the ends should be shaped, what the voltage should be and how to prevent the infuriating hissing noise they made. Hertha published her results in a journal called the *The Electrician* and later on collected her articles into a book. She was the first woman ever to give a talk at the Institution of Electrical Engineers and was the first woman elected as a member of this august body of men.

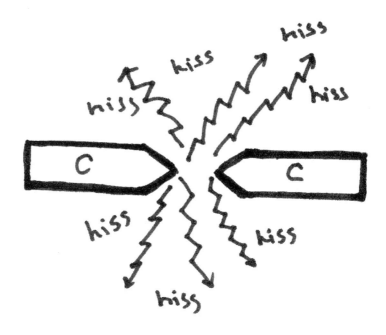

She was also proposed to become a Fellow of the Royal Society: had they elected her she would have been the first woman Fellow. But the Fellows thought only fellows should be Fellows and rejected her. They discussed it like this: 'She is doing good scientific work but we don't want women in our society. What excuse can we find to justify why she cannot join us as a Fellow? Well, she is married, that is a good enough excuse'. And so they declared hat Hertha could not join the fellows because she was a married woman. But they did give her a medal. And later on they let her give a lecture.

Once, when Professor Ayrton was quite ill, and as was the custom then was advised to go to the seaside to recover, Hertha accompanied him. What could she do at the seaside besides caring for her husband? Mary Somerville had collected shells but shell collecting was out of fashion by Hertha's time. She waded into the cold sea, paddled a bit and noticed that the sand under her feet was not smooth but in ridges. These ripples, as she called them, must have been made by the waves. Here is something to investigate! How do these ripples form? So she put sand at the bottom of a glass tub, made waves and watched what happened. She learnt a great deal about how water behaves.

Friendship

1903. Marie and Pierre Curie came to London to tell people about their work on radioactivity which had been recently discovered. In fact it was Marie's idea that radiation in some minerals came from the atoms themselves but Pierre invented the instrument that they used for measuring it. They both got the Nobel Prize. But would the Royal Institution let Marie give a talk? Oh no, it had to be Pierre, but Marie was allowed to listen.

This was when Hertha and Marie met for the first time and the Ayrtons invited the Curies to a party at their house. But it was not the last time the two women met. Fairly soon afterwards Pierre died in a road accident and

Madame Curie (as she is usually called and you can read about her in the book *Dead Famous Scientists*) had quite a rough time in France. Newspapers published unpleasant things about her because she was Polish and because she fell in love with another physicist whose wife became very jealous. When Hertha heard of this she wrote to Marie and invited her for a holiday by the sea. Marie did come to England with her two daughters. She came incognito - which means that she did not want people to know who she was. Instead of using her married name she used her maiden name: Sklodowska. She did not want to meet anyone and just went on long walks on the cliffs. Luckily the journalists did not discover her. With Hertha's help Marie soon felt better and was able to go back home and carry on with her work on radium. Hertha and Marie became really good friends, so when Hertha was invited to talk about her ripples of sand to the French physicists she visited Marie in Paris.

All this was at the time when women were clamouring to be able to vote in the elections. Men did not like this one little bit and these so-called suffragettes had to stage demonstrations and marches. Hertha marched with them. Sometimes the women broke the law in order to get themselves noticed. When Hertha's daughter Barbara (named after Hertha's benefactress) was arrested for smashing the windows of a department store, her mother wrote to a friend that she was 'very proud of her'.

Many others were also put in prison. Some of the women started hunger strikes in prison and were becoming very ill and weak. The government played a 'cat and mouse' game with them: the hunger strikers were let out of prison to get stronger and when they were strong enough they had to go back into prison. Hertha (by then a widow herself) took some of the sick women into her house and nursed them back to health. At Hertha's request Marie Curie (who was by then famous, so her signature counted) signed a petition for suffragettes on hunger strike to be permanently freed. Hertha also made a shady deal with money. When word came that the government was planning to take away the funds of the women's union she took a taxi cab to her bank with the money and deposited it in her own name. Then a few hours later she cashed the same money and sent it abroad. She was doing what could now be called 'money laundering'. Was that correct? And were the suffragettes right to break the law, smash windows for instance. Should one break the law for a cause one believes is just? Think about it.

The Great War (1914-1918)

Madame Curie was busy with her ambulances that carried X-ray machines. (Do you remember Sophia nursing the wounded in Paris more than 40 years earlier?) What could Hertha do? She invented a fan that soldiers in the trenches could use to drive away poisonous fumes. This fan did not use electricity; there was no electricity on the battlefield. It was made of flaps that had to be waved around by hand. In her living room, which was at that time her laboratory, Hertha produced smoke by burning paper and experimented with small model trenches, pillboxes and fans. She also made some experiments with big fans outdoors but had a hard time trying to convince the army of their usefulness. They believed that fans were what ladies waved at parties to cool their faces with. Also, they did not want to train soldiers how to use them. But even so more than a hundred thousand were made and they probably saved many lives.

Not many women have been honoured with a blue plaque.

There is one on the house in Norfolk Square in London where Hertha Ayrton lived and where she experimented in her living room.

Mary

1780 – 1872

Ada

1815 – 1852

Sophia

1850 – 1891

Herta

1854 – 1923

37673107R00032

Printed in Great Britain
by Amazon